KINGFISHER
READERS

level **1**

Baby Animals

Thea Feldman

KINGFISHER

NEW YORK

KINGFISHER
LONDON & NEW YORK

Copyright © Kingfisher 2012
Published in the United States by Kingfisher,
175 Fifth Ave., New York, NY 10010
Kingfisher is an imprint of Macmillan Children's Books, London.
All rights reserved.

Distributed in the U.S. and Canada by Macmillan,
175 Fifth Ave., New York, NY 10010

Library of Congress Cataloging-in-Publication data
has been applied for.

Series editor: Thea Feldman
Literacy consultant: Ellie Costa, Bank Street College, New York

ISBN: 978-0-7534-6754-1 (HB)
ISBN: 978-0-7534-6755-8 (PB)

Kingfisher books are available for special promotions
and premiums. For details contact: Special Markets
Department, Macmillan, 175 Fifth Ave.,
New York, NY 10010.

For more information, please visit
www.kingfisherbooks.com

Printed in China
9 8 7 6 5 4 3 2
2TR/1012/WKT/UNTD/105MA

Picture credits
The Publisher would like to thank the following for permission to reproduce their material. Every care has
been taken to trace copyright holders. However, if there have been unintentional omissions or failure to trace
copyright holders, we apologize and will, if informed, endeavor to make corrections in any future edition.
Top = t; Bottom = b; Center = c; Left = l; Right = r
Cover Shutterstock; Pages 3 Frank Lane Picture Agency (FLPA)/Mitsuako Iwago/Minden; 4 Shutterstock/
Tom Pingel; 5 Shutterstock/Dmitry Pichugin; 6 Shutterstock/Imageman; 7 FLPA/Paul Sawer; 8–9
Shutterstock/Albie Venter; 9 FLPA/Katherine Feng/Minden; 10–11 Shutterstock/Theodore Mattas;
12 FLPA/Hiroya Minakuchi/Minden; 13 Shutterstock/Sergey Uryadnikov; 14 FLPA/Konrad Wothe/Minden;
15 FLPA/Paul Sawer; 16–17 Photolibrary/Peter Arnold Images; 17t Photolibrary/Martin Ruegner;
18 FLPA/Sunset; 19 Shutterstock/Rufous; 20 Alamy/Ashley Cooper; 21 Shutterstock/Ljupco Smokovski;
22 Shutterstock/Pakhnyushcha; 23 FLPA/David Tipling; 24–25 Shutterstock/Kletr; 24b Photolibrary/
Animals Animals; 26 Photolibrary/Imagebroker; 27 Photolibrary/Animals Animals; 28 FLPA/Michael &
Patricia Fogden/Minden Pictures; 29 Shutterstock/Imagestalk; 30–31 Corbis/Ocean

Look!

This dog has babies.

A baby dog is a **puppy**.

Every animal begins life as a baby.

A baby cat is a **kitten**.

A baby cow is a **calf**.

A baby rabbit is a **bunny**.

A baby deer is a **fawn**.

Some baby animals
are big.

baby elephant

Some baby animals
are small.

baby panda

Some baby animals are
born at the same time
as their brothers and sisters.

Lion **cubs** are born together.

Baby killer whales
are born one at a time.

So are baby orangutans.

How are all these
baby animals alike?

They all are cared for
by their mothers.

Some baby animals are fed
by their parents.

These **piglets** get milk
from their mother.

Baby animals need
safe places to stay.

A mother will find a place.

A baby kangaroo is safe
in its mother's pouch!

Do you see how
a baby crocodile stays safe?

It takes a ride
in its mother's mouth!

A baby crocodile begins life inside an egg.

Baby birds **hatch** from eggs too.

Crack!

When it is ready to be born,
a baby chicken hatches
out of the egg.

Ducklings hatch from eggs too.

So does a penguin **chick**.

Some baby animals do not need
to be cared for by their mothers.

Baby spiders do not need care.

Baby snakes do not need care.

Baby turtles hatch ready to go!

So do baby lizards.

Baby frogs are called **tadpoles**.

Do tadpoles look like grown-up frogs?

No.

A grown-up frog looks like this.

Every animal begins
life as a baby.

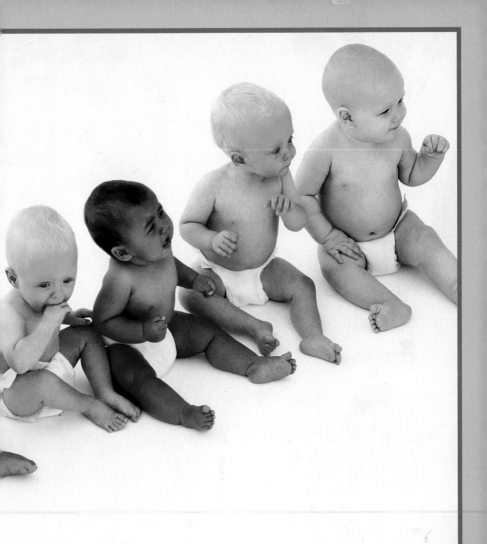

You did too!

Glossary

bunny a baby rabbit

calf a baby cow, elephant or whale, or baby of some other kinds of large animals

chick a baby chicken or penguin, or baby of some other kinds of birds

cubs baby lions or bears, or babies of some other kinds of meat-eating animals

ducklings baby ducks

fawn a baby deer

hatch to break out of an egg and be born

kitten a baby cat

piglets baby pigs

puppy a baby dog

tadpoles baby frogs